Linux

A Comprehensive Guide to Linux Operating System and Command Line

Table of Contents

Introduction

The term Linux refers to an operating system, or kernel, developed by Linus Torvalds and a few other contributors. It was publicly released for the first time in September 1991 and its introduction completely changed how users would experience computing for personal and professional purposes. In a world where Microsoft was charging users for the Windows operating system, Linux was offered to the world as an open-source operating system. This meant that it was free of cost and allowed programmers to customize it as per their requirements. They could use the kernel to create their customized version of an operating system around it. The primary code used for developing the Linux operating system was in the C programming language.

The Linux kernel is used by thousands of operating systems today, and the most popular ones among them comprise Debian, Ubuntu, RedHat, and Fedora. This list is not limited to just the four of these, as new operating systems are developed every year that employ the kernel from the original Linux system.

Mankind reached a milestone in computing technology with Linux's invention and today, Linux powers almost all our devices such as mobiles, laptops, cloud servers, and other supercomputers.

This also led to the creation of a popular job profile known as a Linux System Administrator. The responsibilities of a Linux system admin revolve around the following tasks:

- Knowledge of the Linux file system

- Managing the Linux system's superuser known as Root

- Proficiency in the Linux command line

- Managing users, files, and directories

It is similar to maintaining your personal computer at home but on a larger scale where you are responsible for an entire organization's computer system.

Almost every business today that deals with data and data-related applications uses a Linux based computer known as a server. A Linux server manages all the interactions between a business and its customers, and therefore, it manages huge amounts of customer data. In today's world, data is the new currency and is of utmost importance to a business. If a Linux server is kept down for a long period, it can result in losses worth thousands of dollars for a business. Let us take an example of the shopping giant, Amazon's website. If the

Amazon website went off the Internet even for five minutes, its sales would suffer hugely. This is where Linux knowledge helps and a Linux system admin would save the day. It is the Linux system admin's responsibility to ensure that the Linux system is always up and running and that the website of business never goes off the Internet, even for a second.

This is just one of the many jobs that involves the knowledge and use of the Linux operating system. In the following chapters, we will discuss more about Linux, its origins, its uses, and how it works!

Chapter 1: Features of Linux

Linus Torvalds studied at the University of Helsinki and regularly used Minix, a version of the UNIX operating system. He and a few others realized that a few modifications could make this operating system even more efficient and sent a request to the developer of Minix, Andrew Tanenbaum for these changes. Andrew, however, felt that these changes were irrelevant and discarded their request. This was when Linus decided to create his own operating system that would be developed based on feedback from end-users. He started coding in C language, wrote 95% of Linux in C, and coded the rest in the Assembly language that, at the time, was the second most popular language.

What Kind of Operating System is Linux?

Linux can be classified as a Layered Architecture Operating System, comprising the following layers:

Hardware Layer

This consists of all peripheral devices such as Hard Disk, RAM, CPU, etc.

Kernel

The kernel is the heart of the operating system. It lies between the software and hardware, and all instructions regarding input and output are processed via the kernel.

Shell/GCC

The shell is an interface that lies between the user and the Linux kernel. The shell hides the complexity of the kernel's functions. The shell takes commands from a user as inputs and then instructs the kernel to execute those commands.

Application Software

Software is a utility offered by the operating system so that a user can make maximum use of the operating system's features.

Users

This comprises system users that can interact with the operating system and the application software.

Linux Operating System Features

Linux is a very simple operating system that is free, fast, and easy to use. It is used around the world to power personal computers and laptops. Linux offers the following features:

Live CD/USB

Almost every distribution of the Linux operating system offers a feature known as Live CD/USB. This feature lets you run the entire Linux operating system from a CD or a USB drive without having to install it on the physical hard disk of a computer.

Graphical User Interface

Linux's graphical user interface is known as the X Windows System and is an alternative to the Linux command line. For years, people thought that Linux was only a command-line operating system, but it does offer a neat and user-friendly graphical user interface. Linux has packages that can be installed to make its interface look exactly like the Windows graphical interface.

Support for International Keyboards

Linux is used by people all over the world and therefore, is available in multiple languages. Additionally, it also supports regional keyboard layouts of most countries.

Application Support

Linux maintains a software repository of its own, and users can download and install thousands of applications just by typing a simple command on the Linux shell or terminal. Linux also has support for certain Windows applications if the need arises.

Linux Operating System Characteristics

Linux offers a lot of features, and some of the noteworthy ones are as follows:

Multiuser Support

This is a characteristic of the Linux operating system where the same system, memory, hard disk space, processor, etc. is available to multiple users. This is not made available via a single terminal; instead, there are multiple terminals through which users access these resources. The minimum set of input and output devices for a terminal include the mouse, keyboard, and monitor. The terminals are then connected to the main Linux host machine or Linux server, and the various users can use the resources.

Client/Server architecture is an application of the Linux system's multi-user capability, where numerous clients are connected to the same Linux server. The client will send a request to the server; the server will process it and send the output back to the client. The client terminal is, therefore, also known as a Dumb Terminal.

Multitasking

Linux is capable of processing more than one task in a given instance of time. For example, consider that you have executed a task that sorts through a huge list, and at the same time, you are also typing something in a notepad. These are two simultaneous tasks and Linux will share the CPU time efficiently by implementing scheduling policies such that the CPU will be used for your notepad when you are typing. When you take a break from typing, it will be assigned to the sorting task that you have executed.

Portability

The characteristic that made Linux hugely popular among the masses was portability. Portability, however, does not mean that Linux is smaller in size compared to other operating systems and can be carried around on a CD or USB drive. Portability in Linux refers to the operating system's capability to perform in a similar way across various hardware systems.

Security

Security is a very important aspect of any operating system for a user or an organization that is using the system for their daily work. There are several provisions in Linux to protect its users from unauthorized access to their system and data.

The three main concepts of security in Linux are as follows:

Authentication

This refers to the creation of users and their associated passwords on the Linux operating system. A person cannot access the Linux system unless they have a user and password created for them on the Linux operating system.

Authorization

There are authorization limits set for users on the Linux system at the file and directory level. These deal with permissions such as read, write, and execute. Based on the permissions on a file or a directory, a certain user can read it, make changes to it, or execute the file if it is executable.

Encryption

Linux allows all the files on your operating system to be encoded into an unreadable format known as ciphertext. This ensures that even if someone manages to break into your system, they will not be able to read the data you have on your Linux system's hard disk.

Communication

Linux has an amazing arrangement for communication. Users in the same system can communicate with each other. Moreover, users on different systems connected over a network can also communicate with each other. Data, mail, and even programs can be exchanged between users over a network.

Chapter 2: The Linux Command Line

This chapter will introduce you to the Linux command line and how it can be used to perform different types of tasks on the Linux operating system. When we conclude this chapter, you will know the Linux command line's basic commands that are used to manage files and folders on the Linux system.

The Bash Shell

BASH is short for Bourne-Again Shell. The utility of the Linux operating system helps you interact with the system through Linux commands. When we talk about a command-line utility, we refer to an interface that allows you to give instructions to a computer and its operating system in text mode. There are multiple shell interfaces available today across various Linux-based operating systems, but the most popular one is the bash shell. It is an evolved version of the previously used Linux shell known as the Bourne Shell.

The bash shell will show you a string that indicates it is waiting for the user's input. The string that is displayed is known as the shell prompt. If you are a root user, the shell prompt will end with a # symbol. For a non-root user, it ends with a $.

[root@desktop ~]#

[student@desktop ~]$

To make it easier to understand, the Linux operating system's bash shell is just like the command prompt utility that is available in the Windows operating system. But the scripting language available in the bash shell is much superior compared to the scripting language in the Windows command prompt. We can also compare bash shell to the Power Shell utility that was introduced in Windows 7 and is continued in the versions that followed it. Many professionals have praised the bash shell as a powerful tool for system administration. The scripting language offered in the bash shell can be used to automate numerous tasks in the Linux operating system. Additionally, the bash shell also enables you to perform other complicated tasks that are sometimes not possible via the graphical user interface.

You can access the bash shell using a utility known as the terminal. The keyboard serves as the input to the terminal and the monitor shows the output of your commands. The bash shell can also be accessed using virtual consoles in the Linux system. This lets you have multiple virtual consoles on the base physical console, and every virtual console serves as an individual terminal. Login sessions for multiple users can be created using numerous virtual consoles.

Basics of Shell

The command that you enter on the shell prompt comprises three parts:

1. *Command* that you want to run

2. *Options* that will define the behavior of the command

3. *Arguments* which are the command's targets

The command is a definition of the program that you want to execute. You can have options following the command, or no options at all. The options govern the behavior of the command and they define how the command will function. Options are specified using a dash or two dashes. The dashes are appended so that options can be differentiated from arguments.

Example: -a or –all

Arguments also follow the command on the command prompt and can be again one or more, just like options. Arguments are the targets on which the command will execute.

Let's look at a basic command:

usermod -L John

The command in this example is *usermod*

The option is *-L*

The argument is *John*

This command will lock the password on the system for the user John.

You need to know what options can be used in combination with which commands to effectively use the command line. You can run the *--help* with any command to get a list of options that can be used with a particular command. So, you don't need to know every option that goes with a given command off by heart, and the list will tell you what every option does.

Let us look at what this does when you look up help for the *grep* command. The grep command is used to scan through a file for a string. If the file contains the string specified by you, the output will show all the lines in the file that contain the string.

[student@desktop ~]$ grep --help

Usage: grep [OPTION]... PATTERN [FILE]...

Search for PATTERN in each FILE or standard input.

PATTERN is, by default, a basic regular expression (BRE).

Example: grep -i 'hello world' menu.h main.c

Regexp selection and interpretation:

-E, --extended-regexp PATTERN is an extended regular expression (ERE)

-F, --fixed-strings   PATTERN is a set of newline-separated fixed strings

-G, --basic-regexp   PATTERN is a basic regular expression (BRE)

-P, --perl-regexp   PATTERN is a Perl regular expression

-e, --regexp=PATTERN   use PATTERN for matching

-f, --file=FILE   obtain PATTERN from FILE

-i, --ignore-case   ignore case distinctions

-w, --word-regexp   force PATTERN to match only whole words

-x, --line-regexp   force PATTERN to match only whole lines

-z, --null-data   a data line ends in 0 byte, not newline

Miscellaneous:

-s, --no-messages   suppress error messages

-v, --invert-match   select non-matching lines

-V, --version   display version information and exit

--help   display this help text and exit

Output control:

-m, --max-count=NUM   stop after NUM matches

-b, --byte-offset   print the byte offset with output lines

-n, --line-number   print line number with output lines

--line-buffered   flush output on every line

-H, --with-filename   print the file name for each match

-h, --no-filename   suppress the file name prefix on output

--label=LABEL   use LABEL as the standard input file name prefix

-o, --only-matching   show only the part of a line matching PATTERN

-q, --quiet, --silent   suppress all normal output

--binary-files=TYPE assume that binary files are TYPE;

    TYPE is 'binary', 'text', or 'without-match'

-a, --text   equivalent to --binary-files=text

-I   equivalent to --binary-files=without-match

-d, --directories=ACTION how to handle directories;

    ACTION is 'read', 'recurse', or 'skip'

-D, --devices=ACTION   how to handle devices, FIFOs and sockets;

    ACTION is 'read' or 'skip'

-r, --recursive   like --directories=recurse

-R, --dereference-recursive

    likewise, but follow all symlinks

--include=FILE_PATTERN

    search only files that match FILE_PATTERN

--exclude=FILE_PATTERN

    skip files and directories matching FILE_PATTERN

--exclude-from=FILE   skip files matching any file pattern from FILE

--exclude-dir=PATTERN directories that match PATTERN will be skipped.

-L, --files-without-match print only names of FILEs containing no match

-l, --files-with-matches print only names of FILEs containing matches

-c, --count   print only a count of matching lines per FILE

-T, --initial-tab   make tabs line up (if needed)

-Z, --null   print 0 byte after FILE name

Context control:

-B, --before-context=NUM print NUM lines of leading context

-A, --after-context=NUM print NUM lines of trailing context

-C, --context=NUM   print NUM lines of output context

-NUM   same as --context=NUM

  --group-separator=SEP use SEP as a group separator

  --no-group-separator use empty string as a group separator

  --color[=WHEN],

--colour[=WHEN]   *use markers to highlight the matching strings;*

> *WHEN is 'always', 'never', or 'auto'*

-U, --binary   *do not strip CR characters at EOL (MSDOS/Windows)*

-u, --unix-byte-offsets report offsets as if CRs were not there

> *(MSDOS/Windows)*

'egrep' means 'grep -E'. 'fgrep' means 'grep -F'.

Direct invocation as either 'egrep' or 'fgrep' is deprecated.

When FILE is -, read standard input. With no FILE, read . if a command-line

-r is given, - otherwise. If fewer than two FILEs are given, assume -h.

Exit status is 0 if any line is selected, 1 otherwise;

if any error occurs and -q is not given, the exit status is 2.

Report bugs to: bug-grep@gnu.org

GNU Grep home page:
<http://www.gnu.org/software/grep/>

General help using GNU software:
<http://www.gnu.org/gethelp/>

The syntax of the command prompt can be difficult to understand initially. Once you get used to the following conventions, understanding the command syntax will get easier:

- Options are wrapped in square brackets []

- If you follow a command with ... it indicates the arbitrary length list of the items belonging to that type

- If there are multiple items separated by a pipe | it means that you can specify only one of them

- Angle brackets <> are used to specify variables. So, if you see <filename>, you should know that you have to replace it with the filename of your requirement

Let us look at an example:

[student@desktop ~]$ date --help

date [OPTION]... [+FORMAT]

This indicates that the command is **date** and it takes the options represented by **[OPTION]**. It also takes another option **[FORMAT]** prefixed with a + sign.

Executing Commands on the Bash Shell

The bash shell's main function is to interpret commands input by the user on the command prompt, and then to convert them to instructions for the Linux system. We have already learned the string's syntax that you enter on the command prompt is divided into three parts - command, options, and arguments. You have to use a blank space to separate each word that you enter on the command prompt. The command that you type already has a program defined for it in the Linux system, and then there are options and arguments to customize the command.

Let us go through some common commands that are used in a Linux operating system daily:

The **date** command displays the current date and time of your Linux system. This command can also be used if you want to set a new date and time. You can pass an argument with the + sign for the date command if you want the command's output to be shown in a particular format.

[student@desktop ~]$ date

Sat Aug 5 08:15:30 GMT 2019

[student@desktop ~]$ date +%R

08:15

[student@desktop ~]$ date +%x

08/05/2019

The **passwd** command is used to change the password of a system user. This command requires you to enter the current password of the user to set a new password. The Linux system demands a strong password that will comprise letters in uppercase and lowercase, symbols, and numbers. Additionally, the password that is being set cannot be a dictionary word. A regular user can use the command to change their password only. The root user has the power to change the password for any user on the Linux system.

[student@desktop ~]$ passwd

Changing password for user student.

Changing password for student.

(current) UNIX password: type old password here

New password: Specify new password here

Retype new password: Type new password again

passwd: all authentication tokens updated successfully.

Unlike Windows, there are no file formats or file extensions specified in the Linux file system. However, you can use the **file** command to find out the format of any file. You need to pass the file as an argument to the file command.

[student@desktop ~]$ file /etc/passwd

/etc/passwd: ASCII text

If you pass a folder/directory as an argument to the file command, the output will tell you that it is a directory.

[student@desktop ~]$ file /home

/home: directory

The commands **head** and **tail** help you print the first ten lines or the last ten lines of a file. Both these commands also support the option **-n** that can be used to specify the custom number of lines you want to display.

[student@desktop ~]$ head /etc/passwd

This will print the first 10 lines of the passwd file.

[student@desktop ~]$ tail - n4 /etc/passwd

This will print the last 4 lines of the passwd file.

The **wc** command, when passed with a file as an argument, will count the number of words, lines, and characters in that file. It supports the options **-l, -w, -c** which stand for lines, words, and characters respectively.

[student@desktop ~]$ wc /etc/passwd

30   75   2009 /etc/passwd

This indicates that the passwd file has 30 lines, 75 words, and 2009 characters.

As seen, if you used the wc command without any option, it shows the output for all three options. If you want the output only for a particular option, you can pass that specific option with the wc command.

The **history** command will display all the commands you have used previously, and a number for the command. If you used the ! symbol with the command number, you will see the entire command typed along with the output printed for it.

[student@desktop ~]$ history

1 clear

2 who

3 pwd

[student@desktop ~]$!3

/home/student

As you can see, the !3 expands to the pwd command that was typed by the user that gave the output for the user's present working directory as /home/student.

You can navigate through the output given by the history command using the arrow keys on the keyboard. The commands on top can be accessed using the up arrow key, and the commands below can be accessed using the down arrow key. The left and right arrow keys can be used to edit the command that you are currently on.

File Management Using Command Line

In this section, we will learn commands in the Linux system that you can use to manage files and directories. You will learn commands that will let you move, copy, create, delete, and organize files and directories.

Linux File System Hierarchy

Let us understand the file system hierarchy in a Linux operating system. The Linux file system is a tree that starts from the root and branches downwards to form the other parts of the file system hierarchy. This is an inverted tree as it branches downwards to directories and subdirectories that extend from the root directory.

The root directory is represented as / and sits at the top of the Linux file system hierarchy. The / character represents the root directory and the file and directory paths in the Linux system. For example, **var** which is a subdirectory of the root directory is denoted as /var. Similarly, the var directory has another subdirectory called **log** which is denoted as /var/log.

The root directory has standard sub-directories that are responsible for storing specific files. For example, the /boot subdirectory will have all the required files for when the Linux system boots up.

Let us go through the standard subdirectories under the root directory:

/usr

The software libraries that are shared among all users are stored in this directory. It is further divided into the following important directories:

/usr/bin: User command files

/usr/sbin: Commands used in system administration

/usr/local: Files of software that have been customized locally

/etc

This directory has all the system configuration files in it.

/var

Dynamically changing files such as log files, databases, etc. are stored in this directory.

/run

Files that are created during runtime since the last boot are stored in this directory. The files will get recreated on the next system boot.

/home

This is the home directory for all the users on the Linux system. Users can store their data and other files inside their respective home directories. One user will not have access to another user's home directory.

/root

This is the root user's home directory and no one except the root user may have access to it.

/tmp

Temporary files are stored in this directory. Files in this directory that are older than 10 days and have not been accessed, get deleted automatically. There is another such directory at /var/tmp where files that have not been accessed for 30 days, get deleted automatically.

/dev

This directory has files that reference to hardware devices on the Linux system.

Managing Files and Directories

When we talk about file management, we refer to the creation, deletion, and modification of files on the Linux system. The same set of actions can be performed on directories as well.

Let us go through a set of common commands that you should know to manage files and directories in the Linux system:

Activity	Single Source	Multiple Source
Copy file	cp file1 file2	cp file1 file2 file3 dir
Move file	mv file1 file2	mv file1 file2 file3 dir
Delete file	rm file1	rm -f file1 file2 file3
Create directory	mkdir dir	mkdir -p par1/par2/dir
Copy directory	cp -r dir1 dir2	cp -r dir1 dir2 dir3 dir4
Move directory	mv dir1 dir2	mv dir1 dir2 dir3 dir4
Delete directory	rm -r dir1	rm -rf dir1 dir2 dir3

Let us now go through these file management commands one by one to see how they work:

Directory Creation

The **mkdir** command can be used to create directories or subdirectories. If the directory's name already exists, or if you have not specified the parent directory for your sub-directory properly, you will see errors. If you specify the mkdir command with the **-p** option, it will create parent directories if they do not exist. Therefore, it is important to be careful while using the -p command as you may create unnecessary directories if you enter incorrect spellings and paths.

[student@desktop ~]$ mkdir Drawer

[student@desktop ~]$ ls

Drawer

As you can see, the command created a new directory called Drawer in the student user's home directory.

[student@desktop ~]$ mkdir -p Thesis/Chapter1

[student@desktop ~]$ ls -R

Thesis   thesis_chapter1

In the above example with the option -p, you will notice that the directory Thesis and its subdirectory chapter1 were created at the same time.

Copying Files

The **cp** command is used to copy files in the Linux system. You can copy one or more files, and the syntax also lets you copy one file to another file in the same directory, or to a file in a different directory.

Note: The destination file specified by you should be unique. If you specify an existing file, the contents of that file will be overwritten.

[student@desktop ~]$ cd Documents

[student@desktop Documents]$ cp one.txt two.txt

The above example demonstrates how the content of one.txt is copied to two.txt

[student@desktop ~]$ cp one.txt Documents/two.txt

This example demonstrates how the content of one.txt was copied to two.txt that is located in a different directory.

Moving Files

The **mv** command can be used for moving files, along with an additional operation. If you are using the mv command within the same directory, it will perform a rename on the file. However, if you are using the mv command for a file and specify another directory as the destination, it will move that file to the destination directory.

Note: If the file size is huge, it may take more time to move the file from one directory to another.

[student@desktop ~]$ ls

Hello.txt

[student@desktop ~]$ mv Hello.txt Bye.txt

[student@desktop ~]$ ls

Bye.txt

In the above example, since the mv operation was in the same directory, it just renamed the file Hello.txt to Bye.txt

[student@desktop ~]$ ls

Hello.txt

[student@desktop ~]$ mv Hello.txt Documents

[student@desktop ~]$ ls Documents

Hello.txt

In this example, the mv command destination was another directory and therefore, the file Hello.txt was moved from the user's home directory to the Documents subdirectory.

Deleting Files and Directories

You can use the **rm** command to delete files and directories. Directories can be deleted using the **rm -r** command which deletes the directory, its subdirectories, and all the files in that path.

Note: Unlike Windows, the Linux operating system does not maintain anything like a recycle bin from where deleted files can be restored. Once deleted using the rm command, files and directories cannot be restored. They are deleted permanently.

[student@desktop ~]$ ls

File1.txt Directory1

[student@desktop ~]$ rm file1

[student@desktop ~]$ ls

Directory1

[student@desktop ~]$rm -r Directory1

[student@desktop ~]$ ls

[student@desktop ~]$

The above example demonstrates how files and directories can be deleted using the rm and rm -r command.

Do note that a command called rmdir can be used to delete a directory if there are no files or subdirectories in that directory.

Chapter 3: User/Group Management and File Permissions

In this chapter, we will learn about the users and groups in Linux. We will discuss user management and password policies for the users. By the end of this chapter, you will know the role of users and groups in a Linux system, and how the operating system interprets them. You will learn to create, modify, lock, and delete users and groups that have been created locally on your Linux system. You will also learn about file permissions for a group, and how access can be controlled to files and directories.

Users and Groups

This section will cover users and groups and their association with the Linux operating system.

Who is a User?

Every process or task on the Linux system runs as a user, and every file is under the ownership of a specific user. A user can restrict access to a file or directory. This means that if a process is running as a user, the files and directories the process has access to will also be determined by the user.

You can use the **id** command to get details about the user that is currently logged in to the system. You can also pass another user as an argument to the id command to get basic details for that specific user.

You can use the **ls -l** command to get details of the user that is associated with a file or directory. The third column for the output of the ls -l command will give you the user who owns that file or directory.

The **ps** command can be used to get information for a process. The ps command's default output gives you a list of all processes running in the current shell. You can use the **ps a** command to get a list of all processes running in the entire system. If you want to know the user who owns an ongoing process, you can use the **ps u** command to list the user who owns the process in the first column.

The outputs will display the users by their names, but the Linux system has a UID user ID to track the internal users. The Linux system maintains a database where the usernames are mapped to a number. There is a flat-file located at /etc/passwd which stores the information for all users. This file has seven fields, which are as follows:

username: password: UID: GID: GECOS: /home/dir: shell

Let's discuss these fields in brief:

username: This is a text-based name for the user which is mapped to a UID.

password: Passwords for users were stored here in the past but now they are stored in a different location at /etc/shadow.

UID: This is a unique numeric ID given to a user so that the operating system can identify a user at the fundamental level.

GID: GID stands for Group ID. It is the primary group for a user in the system.

GECOS: This is a text field that has the fill name for a user by default.

/home/dir: Every user is assigned a home directory in the Linux system. The home directory for a user is stored under this field.

shell: The shell is the program that a user accesses after successfully logging in to the Linux system. For a normal user, this is the program that gives the user a command prompt.

What is a Group?

Just like users, a Linux system has groups with a group name and a GID mapped to the group name. You can find information related to groups in the file at /etc/group.

There are two types of groups. Primary and supplementary. Let us understand the features of these groups:

Primary Group

- Every user belongs to exactly one primary group

- The fourth field in the /etc/passwd file defines the primary group for a local user defined by the group ID GID

- When a user creates a new file, the group owner for that file is the primary group of the user

- The primary group for a user has the same name as the user by default. This group is also a User Private Group (UPG) and the user is the only member of this group

Supplementary Group

- A user can be a member of zero or more supplementary groups

- The local user's primary group is listed in the last field in the file at /etc/group. For local groups, comma-separated values are used to identify the membership of the user. It is located in the last field of the file at /etc/group

- *groupname: password:GID:list, of, users, in, this, group*

- Supplementary groups were introduced so that users could be part of more than one group. This allocated resources and services more easily by just allocating them to the group rather than to individual users

The Superuser

We will cover the Linux superuser known as root in this section. You will learn how to complete access to the Linux system by being the superuser or the root user.

Every operating system has a superuser that has all the access and rights to the system. If you have been a Windows user, you may already know about the Windows superuser known as the *administrator*. This superuser is known as **root** in a Linux system. The root user can override everything on the system and is generally used for system administration. Tasks such as installing new software, removing existing software, files, and directory management, etc. can be performed by the root user.

Even devices on an operating system can only be managed by the root user, with a few exceptions. A normal user can manage removable devices such as a USB drive. A normal user can therefore make changes to files and directories on a removable storage device. However, modifications to files and directories on a fixed storage device can only be done by the root user.

With all the unlimited powers that a root user has, they can also damage the system. A root user can delete files and directories, modify user accounts or delete them, create system backdoors, etc. If the root account is compromised, an attacker can take full control over the system. Therefore, it is always advisable that you create normal users and escalate privileges to the root user only when needed.

Managing User Accounts

In this section, you will learn to create and modify user accounts in the local system. User accounts can be managed through a list of Linux commands. Let us go through these commands one by one.

useradd username

This command creates a new user with the username that is passed as an argument. It also applies all the default properties to the new user in the /etc/passwd file if you run the command without any explicit options. The default command will also not set a password for the new user. Therefore, a password needs to be set before the user can log in to the system.

You can type the useradd --help command to see all the options that can be used with the command. Using these options, you can override the default properties set by the useradd command.

usermod –help

This command will display all the options that can be used with the usermod command to make modifications to existing users. Let us go through these in brief.

-c, --comment	This option is used to add a value such as full name to the GECOS field
-g, --gid GROUP	The primary group of the user can be specified using this option

-G, --groups	Associate one or more supplementary groups with user
-a, --append	The option is used with the -G option to add the user to all specified supplementary groups without removing the user from other groups
-d, --home HOME_DIR	The option allows you to modify a new home directory for the user
-m, --move-home	You can move the location of the user's home directory to a new location by using the -d option
-s, --shell	The login shell of the user is changed using this option
-L, --lock	Lock a user account using this option
-U, --unlock	Unlock a user account using this option

userdel username

This command is used to delete the user from the /etc/passwd file. Do note, however, that this command does not delete the user's home directory.

Id

This command will display the current user's properties that are set in the /etc/passwd file including the UID and group details.

id username will display the user's properties that you have passed as an argument to the command.

passwd username

This command can be used to set a new password for a new user, or to modify the password for an existing user. The root user can set the password of any other user to any value. There will be a warning if the password criteria are not met, but the root user can just type the same password again to set it for the other user. In the case of a regular user, the passwd command can be used to change their password only, but all of the password policies have to be met.

UID Range

Specific number ranges are reserved for specific users in Linux.

- UID 0 is always assigned to the root user.

- The system assigns UID 1-200 to system processes in a static manner.

- UID 201-999 is assigned to the system processes that do not own any file in the system.

They are dynamically assigned whenever installed software requests for a process. UID 1000+ are assigned to regular users of the system.

Managing Group Accounts

This section will take you through the creation, modification, and deletion of local group accounts.

If you want to add users to a group, the group must already exist. There are several command-line tools to manage local groups in Linux. Here, we will go through these commands one by one:

groupadd groupname

This command will create a group with the specified group name and assign default properties to the group. It assigns the next available group ID (GID) to the group and stores it in the file at /etc/login.defs. You can also use the **-g** option with the groupadd command to specify a custom GID.

[student@desktop ~]$ sudo groupadd -g 5001 Bteam

The **-r** option will create a system-specific group and assign it a GID that is reserved for system groups.

[student@desktop ~]$ sudo groupadd -r moderators

groupmod

This command is used to modify the properties of an existing group, such as changing the groupname. The group name can be changed by using the **-n** option with the command and passing a new name as an argument.

[student@desktop ~]$ sudo groupmod -n moderators admins

You can use the **-g** option with the command if you want to change the GID of the group.

[student@desktop ~]$ sudo groupmod -g 5005 Bteam

Groupdel groupname

This command will delete the group.

[student@desktop ~]$ sudo groupdel Bteam

Using the groupdel command may not work on a user's primary group.

Usermod

This command can be used to modify the group membership of a user. This can be achieved as follows by using the syntax *usermod -g groupname username*

[student@desktop ~]$ sudo usermod -g student

If you want to add a user to a supplementary group, you can use the syntax *usermod -aG groupname username*

[student@desktop ~]$ sudo usermod -aG wheel student

The option -aG ensures that all modifications are done in append mode. Failing to use it will add the user to the specified group and remove them from all other groups.

Linux File System Permissions

File permissions are a Linux system feature through which access to files by a user can be managed and controlled.

There are three types of users to which file permissions can be applied. They are as follows:

1. user

2. group

3. other

User permissions override group permissions and group permissions override other permissions. The types of permissions applied to a file or a directory are as follows:

1. read

2. write

3. execute

Let us understand the effects of these permissions on files and directories.

Permission	Effect on Files	Effect on Directories
r (read)	Read access to file content	The filenames in a directory can be listed.
w (write)	Write access to file content	The files in the directory can be created or deleted.
x (execute)	The file can be executed as a command	The files in the directory can be accessed subject to the permission of the file itself.

By default, a user will have a read and execute permission to any file so that they can read the file and execute it if it is an executable file. If the user only has read access to the file, they can only read the file and not modify it. If a user has only executed permissions to a file, they will not have access to list the file and will need to know the filename beforehand to run and execute an action on it.

Suppose a user has write permissions to a directory. In that case, they can delete any file in it, regardless of their permissions over the files in the directory.

You can use the **ls -l** command to list files and directories along with the associated ownership and permissions.

[student@desktop ~]$ ls -l test

-rw-rw-r--. 1 student 0 Feb 5 15:45 test

You can use the **ls -l directoryname** command to list a specific directory's contents with information about ownership and permission. If you only want to see a listing of a directory and its properties without its contents, you can use the **-d** option.

[student@desktop ~]$ ls -ld /home

drwxr-xr-x. 5 root   4096 Feb 8 17:45 /home

The Linux Read permission is equivalent to the Windows List Folder Contents permission.

The Linux Write permissions are equivalent to the Windows Modify permission.

The root user permissions in Linux is equivalent to Full Control permission in Windows.

Using the Command Line to manage File System Permissions

This section will show you how you can use the Linux command line to manage file system permissions and ownerships for a file.

The **chmod** command can be used to change the permissions of files in Linux. chmod is short for change mode, since permissions are also referred to as a file or directory mode. The syntax of this command is followed by instructions that make the changes accordingly. There are two ways of changing permissions in Linux, numerically, and symbolically.

Let us look at the symbolic method first. The syntax looks like this:

chmod WhoWhatWhich files|directory

- Who is the user u, group g, other o and a for all

- What is + to add, - to remove, = to set exactly

- Which are r for read, w for write, and x for execute

The letter is used to specify different groups that you want to change the permission for. u is for the user, g is for the group, o is for other, and a is for all.

It is not necessary to specify a new set of permissions for a file while using the symbolic method. You can simply modify the existing permissions by using three symbols, +, -, and = to append permissions to an existing set of permissions.

The permissions' actual values are represented using the letters r for read, w for write, and x for execute.

Let us look at the numerical method next. The syntax for the numeric method looks like:

chmod ### files|directory

- Every position of the # represents an access level viz. User, group, and other

- # is the sum of read r=4, write w=2, execute x=1

3 digits are used in this method to set up permissions for files and directories, and sometimes 4 when special permissions come into the picture. A single digit's possibilities are between 0-7, showing the combinations we can have to read, write, and execute values.

If you can understand the relation between the symbolic and numeric mapping, you will learn to do the conversions too. The numeric representation uses three digits where each digit represents permissions for one of the three groups. If we start from left to right, the first bit is for the user, the middle one is for the group, and the third one is for others. For each group, a combination of read, write, and execute numeric values that can be used are 4, 2, and 1 respectively.

The symbolic representation of permissions for a file or directory looks like **-rwxr-x---**

If we look at the example, **-rwxr-x---**

- The user has read write and execute permissions **rwx.** Converting this to numeric form would give you r4 + w2 +x1 which is a total of 7.

- The group has only read **r** and execute **x** permissions. Converting this to numeric form would give you r4 + x1 which is a total of 5.

- The permissions for others is --- In numeric terms, the value is 0.

If we convert this entirely into the numeric form, the value would be **750**.

Chapter 4: Linux Vs. Windows

MAC and Linux are both Unix type operating systems and therefore, we will not be discussing the comparisons between MAC and Linux. Moreover, there are only two contenders, Linux and Windows, when it comes to global server architecture. Commercially, no business has ever tried using a MAC operating system as a server.

Linux is widely regarded as being a better operating system than Windows, and we will discuss the advantages of Linux over Windows in this chapter.

If you have never used a Linux operating system before, you may already have a bias towards Windows. However, in reality, Linux holds a lot of benefits over Windows.

Let us look at the advantages of Linux over Windows one by one:

Open Source Nature

Purchasing a Windows operating system is like buying a car that you do not have complete control over and cannot modify it as per your requirements. In contrast to this, Linux is an open-source operating system. This means you have 100%

access to the source code of the entire operating system. This means that you can make any number of tweaks to the operating system and make it work in whatever manner you require it to.

Many people, mostly everyday users, do not care for an operating system's open-source nature, but it is the most important feature to have at an industrial level.

Secure

The Windows operating system is vulnerable and has multiple flaws that attackers and hackers exploit every day. Linux on the other hand is not as vulnerable as Windows. It has its own set of loopholes but is very secure compared to Windows.

The functions of the Linux operating system are what makes it secure. The process of package management, repositories, control on the command line, and a few other features empower Linux to be a much more secure operating system than Windows.

When you have a Windows operating system on your machine, you also need to purchase antivirus software to secure your machine against attackers and hackers. There no such necessity for antivirus software with Linux. There are a few antivirus tools available for Linux as well but you don't really need them.

Linux's default secure nature makes the experience comfortable for you and helps you save money as you do not have to invest in premium antivirus software.

Revives Old Computers

The hardware requirements for a system increase exponentially as operating systems keep evolving. For example, if you were to purchase the latest version of Windows 10 today, you would need to ensure that your system meets the minimum hardware requirements to run the Windows 10 operating system. You cannot run it on a system with sub-standard hardware.

But that is not the case with Linux. You could pick up even a decade old system and install Linux on it. This does not mean that you would install any Linux distribution on a system with an old processor and a 256 MB RAM. However, Linux has multiple distributions that you can install on low-end systems, such as Puppy Linux.

We can say that there is a range of Linux distributions available that can be fitted from high-end to low-end systems. In comparison, Windows does not offer such flexibility.

Overall, if you compare a high-end Windows system to a high-end Linux system, the Linux system will have the edge over Windows when it comes to performance. This is one of the many reasons that there are more Linux-based servers in the world today as compared to Windows.

Programmer Friendly

Linux supports all the major programming languages available today such as C, C++, Java, Python, Ruby, Perl, etc. Additionally, it comes equipped with a variety of applications that prove useful for programming purposes.

Developers have always found the Linux terminal far superior to the Windows command prompt in terms of functionality. There are many native libraries for Linux in the Linux terminal. Programmers have also pointed out that it is easier to manage tasks with the package manager available in Linux.

Bash scripting is another major reason why programmers prefer Linux to Windows.

Linux also offers native support for SSH which is used for server management. There are several commands on the Linux command line that make Linux an obvious choice of an operating system for servers as compared to Windows.

Software Updates

Microsoft pushes a software upgrade for Windows whenever it learns of a major problem that needs fixing. This means that an update may break your system experience, or you may need to wait for a significant amount of time for an update to fix your system. If you have used a Windows-based operating system over the years, you would know that Windows updates often end up causing more issues than they fix.

However, with Linux, you will see that software updates roll out to patch the smallest of bugs and don't break your system. Linux, therefore, uses fast and effective updates to fix your problems. This is not the case with Windows, unfortunately.

Customization

The biggest advantage of using a Linux operating system over Windows is customization. If you like to play around and tweak your operating system's looks and functionality, Linux is the perfect operating system for you.

Linux offers a ton of themes and icons, and it is not just the graphical aspect of the Linux operating system that you can customize. You can customize the Linux binaries by merely changing a few lines of code to make an application work as per your needs.

Multiple Distributions

Windows does not come in multiple flavors, but it does offer different packages and plans concerning the licensing activation period, inbuilt software, and price.

As opposed to this, there are hundreds of Linux distributions available to cater to specific needs. So based on their requirements, a user can choose between hundreds of Linux distributions to install on their system and work with.

For example, there are Linux distributions available for ethical hackers, programmers, old computers, children, and the list goes on. There is a Linux flavor for everyone.

Free To Use

The Linux operating system is available to everyone for free. This has not been the case with Windows. You will not have to spend $100 to $200 to procure a Linux based distribution such as Ubuntu, Debian, etc. It is all free.

You end up saving a lot of money when you choose Linux as your operating system, and you can invest those savings in upgrading your system's hardware components instead.

Community Support

If you ever encounter a hurdle while using your Linux operating system, you do not need to hire an expert to fix it. You just need to do a Google search for a Linux community support thread that answers the problem you are facing. You will likely find a thread where someone has faced a similar problem in the past and a solution was discussed for it. If you do not find an existing thread, you can start a new thread by posting your problem, and someone from the Linux community will gladly help you out with a solution. You can typically expect a reply to your query within minutes of posting the thread.

There are a lot of active Linux users on the Internet who are always ready to respond to a query by another Linux user. The number of active members on Linux forums is way more than the number of active members for any Windows-based forums.

Reliability

As we know, Windows tends to get more and more sluggish with every day that passes by. Your computer will start crashing often, or slow down after a few years, and you will need to reinstall Windows to fix the issue.

There is no need to reinstall Linux to improve your user experience, as it works smoothly by default for much longer than a Windows system.

Another pain point of Windows is that you need to reboot the system after any kind of a change.

- Reboot after installing new software

- Reboot after uninstalling software

- Reboot after a Windows update

- Reboot if the system is slow

However, in Linux, you do not need to reboot the system for any of the above reasons. You can continue working and Linux will not demand a reboot from you for these tasks.

Another fact that proves Linux is reliable is its adoption rate for web servers in the world. Almost every Internet giant such as Amazon, Google, and Facebook have their servers running on the Linux operating system. Almost every supercomputer in the world also runs on Linux.

So why does everyone prefer Linux to Windows for mission-critical tasks? The reason is simple. Linux is much more reliable than Windows.

This does not mean Linux has zero issues. But when we look at the bigger picture, Linux has a more reliable design.

Privacy

Microsoft has promised that the data collection it does from every Windows user is anonymous. However, this has not been convincing ever since the release of Windows 10. Microsoft has already received a lot of criticism over data collection, and what it should and shouldn't collect.

If you ever navigate to the privacy settings in Windows 10, you will see that everything is enabled by default. Microsoft will also still collect data from your system even after you opt-out from sending data to them. Microsoft will not admit that they collect data in a press release, but they are collecting data. You need third-party tools to disable the inbuilt spyware that comes with Windows.

If you are concerned about privacy, Linux will be the perfect operating system for you yet again. Linux systems do not collect a lot of data and you will not need any third-party tools to protect your privacy as a Linux user.

Chapter 5: The Linux Kernel

An operating system comprises the following modules:

- Bootloader: This is the software module in charge of the boot process of the operating system

- Kernel: This is the core module of the operating system that sends instructions to the CPU, memory, and other peripheral devices

- Daemons: These are the services that run in the background of the Linux operating system

- Networking: These are communication-related services that send and receive information between devices

- Shell: This is a module for command-line instructions that are input by the user of the Linux system

- Graphical Server: This is the subsystem that displays graphics on your screen

- Desktop Environment: This is the primary point of interaction between a user and the system

- Applications: This is software that performs the tasks executed by the user such as text editors

Kernel Space and Userspace

Kernel Space

The kernel is found in an elevated system state and has a protected memory space. It also has complete access to the system's hardware. The system space and memory space together is known as the kernel space. The core access to the system services and hardware is managed within the kernel space. They are further offered as services to the remaining system.

User Space

The user space is the region where user applications exist and function. In user space, user applications can access a subset of the system's available resources via kernel calls. A user application can be created such as an office software or a game by using the kernel's core services.

The Linux Kernel

The Linux kernel was first officially released on September 17, 1991, and since then it has defied all odds to become the defining component of the Linux system.

A kernel can be of three types: monolithic, microkernel, or hybrid. The Linux kernel is a monolithic kernel. The Linux line of operating systems, popularly known as Linux distributions, have this kernel as their foundation. Unlike the microkernel, the monolithic kernel works through the CPU, memory, and IPC and comprises device drivers, file management systems, and system server calls. The monolithic kernel is the best for communicating with hardware and executing multiple threads at the same time. This is why the reaction rate of Linux processes is so fast.

The Linux kernel has a few drawbacks as well. It requires a huge install and memory footprints. It also has security loopholes as it operates in the supervisor mode. In comparison, microkernels may be slow to address system calls and the kernel and user service operate independently. They are smaller in size as compared to the monolithic kernel. A microkernel can be scaled easily but requires more code to be written to do so. The Linux kernel is written using C and the Assembly programming languages.

Relationship of the Linux Kernel with Hardware

The kernel makes use of a concept known as *interrupts,* to control the system's hardware. When hardware wants to use the system resources, it sends an interrupt to the CPU, sending an interrupt to the kernel. The kernel is capable of disabling interrupts, be it single or multiple, to provide synchronization. The interrupts in Linux do not run in context to processes, but in context to interrupts not associated with any process.

What is different in the Linux Kernel as compared to other UNIX kernels?

There are significant differences between the Linux kernel and other classic UNIX kernels. They are as follows:

- Kernel modules can be loaded dynamically in Linux

- The nature of the Linux kernel is preemptive

- Linux supports symmetric multiprocessors

- Linux is open-source and free

- The Linux kernel ignores the standard features of UNIX, as Linux developers feel they are poorly developed

- Linux is an object-oriented model with device classes, a userspace device filesystem, and events that can be hot-plugged

- The Linux kernel does not differentiate between normal processes and threads

The Linux Kernel Architecture

Components of the Linux Kernel

A kernel is simply a resource manager. The resources it manages can be a process, memory, or hardware device. The kernel manages and distributes resources between users and processes competing for the resources. The Linux kernel is located in the kernel space, right below the user space where user applications are executed. The userspace communicates with the kernel space via a GNI library, enabling the system call interface to connect to the kernel space, and allows a transition back to the userspace.

There are three primary levels of the Linux kernel:

System Call Interface

This is the topmost level of the Linux kernel and is responsible for actions like read and write.

Kernel Code

This level is located below the system call interface. It is common for all server architectures supported by Linux and is, therefore, known as architecture-independent kernel code.

Architecture-dependent Code

This level lies below the architecture-independent code. It forms a level that is usually known as the Board Support Package, or BSF in short. This kernel level contains the bootloader package responsible for initiating the operating system and device drivers into the system memory.

The architectural components of the Linux kernel comprise the following:

System Call Interface

This thin layer lies between the user space and the kernel, taking input function calls from the user and feeding them to the kernel. This interface depends on the architecture.

Process Management

This mainly exists for process management. A process is referred to as a thread in the kernel and represents an individual processor's virtualization.

Memory Management

Memory is managed through pages resulting in efficiency. Linux has functions in place to manage memory as well as hardware for virtual and physical mappings. Linux also features something known as Swap Space that incorporates hard disk space for memory management.

Virtual File System

A virtual file system provides interface abstraction for file systems. A user can switch between the system call interface and file systems using the kernel's virtual file system.

Network Stack

This is a layer that contains all protocols necessary for maintaining a network.

Device Drivers

The Linux kernel has significant source code for device drivers that contain libraries for hardware devices attached to the Linux system.

Architecture-dependent Code

This code has elements that depend largely on architecture and therefore should consider the architecture for proper functioning.

Interfaces

System Calls and Interrupts

Applications use system calls to pass information to the kernel. Applications do this, using libraries that contain specific functions for this task. The libraries then instruct the kernel using the system calls to perform the task demanded by the application.

Interrupts empower the Linux kernel to control the system's hardware. If hardware wants to communicate with the system, it can do so by triggering an interrupt on the processor that is ultimately sent as an interrupt to the Linux kernel.

Linux Kernel Interfaces

The Linux kernel brings many interfaces for userspace applications and these interfaces have various properties and are capable of performing multiple tasks. There are two distinct

Application Programming Interfaces (API) known as the kernel-user space and the kernel internal. The Linux API supports the kernel-user space API and enables applications from the user space to access the kernel's system resources and services. It comprises the subroutines from the GNU C library and the System Call Interface.

Linux ABI

ABI stands for Application Binary Interface and refers to the kernel-user space ABI. The Linux ABI can be defined as the interface that lies between various program modules. The difference between API and ABI is that ABI is used to access externally compiled code, whereas API is a structure that manages software. More than a Linux kernel, an ABI is defined by a Linux distribution. Every architecture requires a specific instruction set such as x86-64. ABI is consumed more than API by end-users of Linux products.

System Call Interface

As discussed previously, the system call interface plays a role in the kernel. It is the denomination and collective of all the system calls.

The C Standard Library

The kernel system calls are a part of the GNU C library. The Linux API is a part of the GNU C library and the system call interface known as Glibc.

Portable Operating System Interface (POSIX)

POSIX is a collective term for standards used for maintaining compatibility between various operating systems. It is responsible for declaring the API bundled with command-line shells and utility interfaces. POSIX defines useful features for the Linux API and also additional features for the kernel such as:

- Cgroups subsystem

- Systems calls of the Direct Rendering Manager

- A feature called readahead

- A Getrandom call

- System calls such as epoll, futex, dnotify, splice, inotify, and fanotify

The Modular Kernel

The initial versions of the Linux kernel were monolithic, such that they had multiple static parts fixed into a single part. However, modern Linux kernels contain multiple modules fed to the kernel dynamically, as and when needed. This is different as compared to the monolithic kernels and are therefore referred to as modular kernels. The advantage of a modular kernel is that code can be loaded as modules in the kernel without rebooting the system.

The Linux Loadable Kernel Module (LKM)

Code can be added to the Linux kernel in the form of modules using the kernel source tree. It is beneficial if code can be added to the kernel while the kernel is running. The modular code is also known as a loadable kernel module. The modules have specific tasks that are divided into three types: system calls, file system drivers, and device drivers.

You can compare the loadable kernel module in Linux to the kernel extensions offered by other operating systems. Modules can be added to the kernel by loading it in the loadable kernel module or appending it to the base kernel.

The loadable kernel module has the following benefits compared to binding code to the base kernel:

- You can save time and avoid errors as you do not need to rebuild the kernel

- System problems such as bugs can be discovered using the loadable kernel module

- The loadable kernel modules save space as you need to load them only when needed

- The maintenance and debugging of loadable kernel modules is fast

Uses of the Loadable Kernel Module

The loadable kernel module has the following uses:

Device Drivers

The kernel uses this module to communicate with the hardware on the system. The device driver needs to be loaded into the kernel before the device can be used.

Filesystem Drivers

These drivers are used to translate the contents of the file system.

System Calls

The applications running in the user space employ system calls to procure services of the kernel.

Network Drivers

These drivers translate network protocols.

Executable Interpreters

These are responsible for loading and managing executable files.

Compiling the Linux Kernel

Contrary to popular opinion, compiling the Linux kernel is a simple task. Let us go through a step by step guide to compiling the Linux kernel. We have used the Fedora 13 KDE distribution for our example. It is advisable to back up your data and GRUB just to ensure that you have a backup if something goes wrong.

1. Download the source code from http://kernel.org/

2. Navigate to downloads directory on the terminal and extract the source code from the download archive using the following command:

   tar xvjf Linux-2.6.37.tar.bz2

3. Clear the build area before compilation by using the command:

   make mrproper

4. Use a configuration like xconfig that will make it easy to run any program.

5. Select the features and modules that you wish for your kernel to have.

6. Generate the .config file and then go to MakeFile.

7. Execute the compilation by running the make command.

8. Install the modules by running the command:

   modules_install

9. Copy the kernel and the system map to the /boot directory.

10. Run the command new-kernel-pkg to build the list of dependencies for the new modules.

That's it. You have compiled your customized Linux kernel in 10 easy steps.

Upgrading the Kernel

The Linux kernel can be easily upgraded from an existing version to a newer version while retaining all the existing version's configuration data. First, you need to create a backup of the kernel's .config file in the kernel's source directory. This is a security measure for the worst-case scenario if something goes wrong. The steps to upgrade the Linux kernel are as follows:

1. Download the latest source code for the Linux kernel from the kernel.org website

2. Make the changes to the old source tree to bring it to the latest version

3. Reconfigure the new kernel by adding the configuration of the old kernel file that you have backed up

4. Build the new kernel

5. You can now install the newly built kernel

Downloading the source code of the new kernel

The Linux kernel source code developers understand that not all users would want to download the entire source code as it may consume disk space and bandwidth. Therefore, they also roll out patches that just upgrade the existing version of a user's kernel. The only thing a user needs to know is which patch file is compatible with their existing kernel version, as a patch file will succeed at upgrading only a specific kernel version. You can apply patch files using the following methods:

- Stable kernel patches that can be applied to base kernel versions.

- Base kernel patches that can be applied only to the previous version of the base kernel.

- An incremental patch upgrade can be used from one release to the next release. This saves developers the trouble of downgrading a kernel and then upgrading it. Using this method, they can simply switch from the current version to the next stable version available for their kernel.

What Can We Conclude About the Linux Kernel?

The Linux kernel is a resource manager, and acts through an abstract layer for the Linux system's applications. The applications use the kernel to interact with the hardware and services of the system. Linux is a multitasking operating system and the Linux kernel is apt for processing multiple tasks. The Linux kernel is open source and highly customizable. Therefore, it can be used with a wide range of devices, unlike other operating systems.

The modular Linux kernel is the icing on the cake. It allows modifications to be made to the kernel without the need to reboot the system.

The monolithic Linux kernel has better processing abilities than a microkernel.

Chapter 6: Introduction to Shell Scripting in Linux

Shell scripting refers to the open-source computer programming language developed for the Linux shell. Shell scripting is nothing but writing a series of Linux commands to be executed automatically. The code for a shell script can be as short as a single line, or it can be lengthy, containing repetitive commands that can be stored in a single script such that the effort to type the commands manually every time is reduced.

In this chapter, we will try to teach you the basics of shell scripting in Linux. We will also discuss some advanced concepts of shell scripting. This chapter aims to discuss how shell scripting works and will serve as a launchpad to the world of shell scripting.

How to Write a Shell Script in Linux

Shell scripts are written using text editors. There are several text editors available on a Linux system such as vi, vim, and nano. You can open any text editor and begin writing a shell script or a shell program. You need to ensure that the file you create for your shell script has execute permissions. And then, you just need to keep the shell script file in a location that is accessible to the Linux shell.

The following are the steps that go into creating a shell script:

1. Create a new file using a text editor like vi. Name the script file and give it a .sh extension.

2. Start the script with the first line as #! /bin/sh

3. Write some Linux commands.

4. Save the file as filename.sh

5. You can execute the script file using the command bash filename.sh

#! Is known as a shebang operator. It directs the script to the location of the interpreter. Therefore, when you specify your shell script's first line as #! /bin/sh, the script is directed to the Bourne shell located at /bin/sh.

Let us try to create a small and simple script:

#!/bin/sh

ls

You can name this script as list.sh

You can run this script using the following command.

[student@desktop ~]$ bash list.sh

Documents Movies Books Pictures

As you can see, the script is simply performing the function of the **ls** function.

Adding Comments to your Shell Script

Commenting is used in shell scripting as in any programming language. The syntax to add a comment is as follows.

#this is a comment

So taking the above script as an example, your script with the comment would look like this.

#!/bin/sh
#this is my first script

Ls

Shell Variables

Variable store data in the form of numbers and characters. Similarly, shell variables also store information that can be accessed by the shell.

For example, the below shell script creates a shell variable and then prints it.

variable ="Hello"

echo $variable

Let us look at another small shell script that uses a variable:

#!/bin/sh

echo "what is your name?"

read name

echo "How do you do, $name?"

read remark

echo "I am $remark too!"

How Does this Script Work?

When you execute this script, you will first be prompted with the question "what is your name?"

You will then get an option to input your name. If you type in John, the string *John* is stored by the program in the variable **name,** and in the next question, the program uses your John that it has stored to give you the new question "How do you do John" where the variable $name is replaced by the name that you entered. The response to this question is also stored in a new variable **remark.** So, if you replied 'excellent', the next statement by the program will replace $remark with it and give you the output "I am excellent too!".

This is a simple script and you can develop much more complex scripts that will have loops, conditional statements, and functions.

Chapter 7: The Linux Boot Process

Have you ever been curious about how your Windows or Linux system boots up and prepares the whole system ready for you? In this chapter, we will discuss the entire boot process for a Linux system, and explain what happens from the time you press the power button until you are presented with your login screen and the desktop.

It is important to understand the boot process and startup process in Linux if you want to get good with its configuration and troubleshoot any issues concerning startup. This chapter will take you through the Linux boot and startup process, focusing mainly on the bootloader utility known as GRUB2, and system initialization Linux process known as systemd.

To start a Linux system, you need a couple of sequences that bring it to a state that is ready for use. This process is initiated when you press the power button and concludes when the Linux kernel is up and the control is passed over to systemd. After systemd is initiated, the startup process takes control and concludes when the Linux system is in a usable state for any user.

The Linux boot and startup sequence are simple to understand. It comprises the following steps, which we will be discussing in detail:

- BIOS POST

- Boot loader (GRUB2)

- Kernel initialization

- Initialize systemd

In this chapter, we will be discussing the boot and startup sequence using GRUB2 and systemd since a majority of Linux distributions work with them. However, there may be a few Linux distributions that still use older software for boot and startup.

The Boot Sequence

There are a couple of ways to initiate the boot sequence in Linux. The first one is as simple as switching your system on, which will trigger the boot sequence. If the system already has a regular user or root user, they can use the command line or the GUI to reboot the system. When you reboot the system, it will first shut down the system and initiate the boot sequence again.

BIOS POST

The primary step of the boot sequence in Linux is not related to Linux at all. This step deals with the system's hardware initiation and is universal across the various operating systems available today. When you press the power button for a computer, the Power On Self Test known as POST is initialized, which is a subset of the Basic Input Output System, known as BIOS in short.

BIOS was developed to initialize hardware when IBM developed the first computer in 1981. POST is a subset of BIOS that ensures that all the hardware functions properly. If the Power On Self Test fails, it is an indication that the system may be unusable and BIOS will not be initiated.

BIOS and POST check the system hardware's simple operation, following it up with a BIOS interrupt called INT 13H. This interrupt finds any bootable device and locates its boot sectors. When it comes across the first valid boot sector containing a valid boot record, it loads it into memory and then the control is passed to the code present in the boot sector.

The boot loader's first stage, therefore, is the boot sector. Linux distributions have used 3 bootloaders over the years, LILO, GRUB, and GRUB2. The latest and most popular boot loader is GRUB2, which is used by almost all Linux distributions today.

GRUB2

GRUB2 is short for GRand Unified Bootloader, version 2. It is now the first choice for bootloader preferred by most Linux distributions. The GRUB2 module makes the computer sufficiently smart to locate the operating system's kernel and load it into memory.

Although Linux has never officially issued any stage notification for GRUB2, it consists of three stages. Let us discuss them further:

Stage 1

As we have discussed in the section for POST and BIOS, when POST concludes, BIOS searches for any attached bootable devices, locates the Master Boot Record (MBR) on it, and then loads it into RAM and the boot record is executed. The bootstrap code's size for stage 1 of GRUB2 is so small it can accommodate itself on the hard disk's first 512-byte sector with the partition table. The maximum disk space allocated to the bootstrap code is about 446 bytes. This stage one file of 446 bytes is called boot.img. The partition table is not a part of this file.

Since the boot record is minuscule, it does not have any information about the file system structure. Therefore, in its first stage, the GRUB2 bootloader is only supposed to locate the next stage. GRUB2 bootloader's stage 1.5 is located between the boot record and the bootable drive's primary partition. After loading stage 1.5 of GRUB2 into the RAM, stage 1.5 takes control.

Stage 1.5

As discussed, stage 1.5 must always lie between the boot record and the bootable device's primary partition. This part of the disk was kept unused for many years for technical purposes. The hard disk drive gets first partitioned during sector 63. The master boot record starts at sector 0. This means that there are 62 sectors, or 512-byte sectors, or simply 31,744 bytes in between, where the core.img file can be stored that contains GRUB2's stage 1.5. The core.img file has a size of 25,389 bytes and evidently, there is more than enough space to store it after the master boot record sector.

As there is enough space to accommodate a lot of code concerning stage 1.5, there is space for additional code to accommodate file system drivers such as EXT, NTFS, and FAT. This means the code for GRUB2's stage 2 can also be kept on a standard EXT file system. The default location of the GRUB2 stage 2 is located at /boot/grub2.

Stage 2

All the necessary files for stage 2 of Grub2 are located at /boot/grub2 and its subdirectories. There is no image file for GRUB2 like in the case of stage 1 and stage 2. Instead, it has kernels that get loaded as and when required from the directory at /boot/grub2/i386-pc.

The purpose of stage 2 of GRUB2 is to detect the Linux kernel and load it into RAM, thereby giving the kernel full control. The files for the Linux kernel are stored in the directory at /boot. It is easy to identify these files as they all begin with **vmlinuz**. The contents of the /boot directory will give you a list of all kernels that are currently installed on your Linux system.

You will get a list of kernels that are installed on your system in GRUB2 stage 2 and selecting one of the kernels will pass the boot process control to the respective kernel.

Kernel

All the kernels today come in a compressed format but also self-extract themselves. The kernel, as discussed, can be found in the directory at /boot. When you select a kernel, it is loaded into RAM, its execution begins and it should extract itself to become a usable format. When the kernel is extracted, it will call **systemd**, and control is passed from the kernel to systemd.

This is where the boot process ends. At this instance in time, both the bootloader and systemd are executing but are useless to the system user as no other application is running.

The Startup Sequence

After the boot sequence concludes, the startup sequence is initiated to ultimately bring the Linux system to a state that is usable by an end-user to perform productive tasks.

Systemd

The Linux system's fundamental process is systemd and is responsible for starting the Linux system and bring it to a usable state for an end-user. Before systemd, Linux systems used a service known as **init**. Compared to init, the functions of systemd are vast as they can handle countless areas of a Linux system such as mounting file systems, initiating and managing services concerning the system processes, and more.

First, systemd will mount all the file systems that are defined in the configuration file at /etc/fstab. It also has access to all the configuration files at /etc.

The configuration file located at /etc/systemd/system/default.target is read to figure out which target or state the system should be booted into. For a personal desktop, this is usually the **graphical.target**. For a Linux system that is a server, the default target is usually a **multi-user.target**.

Services and targets are units of the systemd service. Every target has some dependencies for it that are defined in their configuration files. Systemd also starts the dependencies of the target. The dependencies imply services that are required to operate the Linux system as per the target that was initiated. When the target's dependencies are loaded and the system is up and running, we can say that the Linux system is functioning in that target mode.

The checkpoints of the startup process are the two targets, **sysinit.target,**   followed by the **basic.target**. Although systemd is known to start services simultaneously, some services need to be initiated before all the other services and targets are initialized. The system cannot pass a checkpoint until all the targets and services required by a particular checkpoint are started.

The sysinit.target will start after all its dependencies have been initialized. There are multiple tasks concerning the dependencies of sysinit.target and they are performed in parallel inside of sysinit.target.

The sysinit.target will initialize all the smaller services that are essential to move on to basic.target. The basic target has some extra functions that are initialized to reach the next target. These comprise setting up of paths to executables, communication sockets, etc.

After all, this is done, the **graphical.target** or **multi-user.target** can be initialized. However, note that it is important that the multi-user.target is reached before the dependencies for the graphical target are reached.

If your system's default target is multi-user.target, you will see a text input prompt login for you to log in to the console. Linux servers that run without a graphical interface usually have their default target as multi-user.target. If you have installed Linux on your system and included the GNU Desktop graphical user interface, setting the default target as graphical.target will take you to a graphical login.

This is the end of the startup sequence. You can now enter your username and password to log in to the system.

GRUB2 and systemd are the boot process's core components and the startup process for any modern-day Linux system. These two key parts work hand in hand to load the Linux kernel and then start all the other services needed to make a Linux system usable for the end-user.

Conclusion

Linux is a very secure system and is therefore used by businesses all over the world today. User data is the most expensive entity today, and therefore, any compromise in data can amount to huge losses for an organization. Linux has proved to be a very secure operating system for a business to run its applications and store customer data. The open-source nature of the Linux operating system ensures that security patches are rolled out faster for Linux than any other operating system in the world today. This has made Linux the ideal platform for any business concerning security. Many other features offered by Linux are unparalleled by other operating systems.

This book is an introduction into the Linux world, and I hope that it encourages you to look at advanced learning options in the Linux domain!